ROCK Records

By Jan Mike

Series Literacy Consultant
Dr Ros Fisher

PEARSON
Longman

Pearson Education Limited
Edinburgh Gate
Harlow
Essex CM20 2JE
England

www.longman.co.uk

The rights of Jan Mike to be identified as the authors of this Work have been asserted by her in accordance with the Copyright, Designs and Patents Act, 1988.

Text Copyright © 2004 Pearson Education Limited. Compilation Copyright © 2004 Dorling Kindersley Ltd.
All rights reserved. No part of this publication may be reproduced, stored in a retrieval system or transmitted in any form or by any means electronic, mechanical, photocopying, recording, or otherwise, without either the prior written permission of the publishers and copyright owners or a licence permitting restricted copying in the United Kingdom issued by the Copyright Licensing Agency Ltd., 90 Tottenham Court Road, London W1P 9HE

ISBN 0 582 84142 9

Colour reproduction by Colourscan, Singapore
Printed and bound in China by Leo Paper Products Ltd.

The Publisher's policy is to use paper manufactured from sustainable forests.

DK
The following people from **DK** have
contributed to the development of this product:

Art Director Rachael Foster
Martin Wilson **Managing Art Editor** | **Managing Editor** Marie Greenwood
Rebecca Johns **Design** | **Editorial** Patricia Moss, Selina Wood
Alison Prior **Picture Research** | **Production** Gordana Simakovic
Richard Czapnik, Andy Smith **Cover Design** | **DTP** David McDonald
Consultants Keith Lye

Dorling Kindersley would like to thank Chanele Dandridge and Alastair Muir; Rose Horridge, Hayley Smith and Gemma Woodward in the DK Picture Library; Johnny Pau for additional cover design work.

Illustrations: Colin Rose, Colin Salmon. **Picture Credits:** Alamy Images: Randa Bishop 18bl. Corbis: Morton Beebe 31tr; Bettmann 20bl; Jonathan Blair 6b; Robert Garvey 1; Charles O'Rear 6t; Roger Ressmeyer 7br; Kevin Schafer 36bc; Bill Stormont 28-29b; Michael S. Yamashita 37bl. DK Images: British Museum 5tr; Hunterian Museum 26tr; National Museum of Wales 36t; Natural History Museum 3br, 17cra, 17clb, 17bl, 19r, 23cra, 27b; Sedgwick 24tr; State Museum of Nature 35cra. N.H.P.A.: John Shaw 34br. Tom Pantages: 30b. Science Photo Library: Jeremy Bishop 13bl; Dee Breger 31bl; Simon Fraser 21b; Adam Jones 4b; James King-Holmes 29tr; Martin Land 20cl; Dr Kari Lounatmaa 26br; NASA 14tl; David Parker 12tl; Ph. Plailly/ Eurelios 22tr; Sinclair Stammers 22clb, 22br. J & B Sibbick: 24bl. Tony Waltham Geophotos: 16b; Colin Rose and Colin Salmon for illustrations; Jacket: Honolulu Star-Bulletin: George F. Lee front bl. Science Photo Library: Adam Jones back.

All other images: **DK** Dorling Kindersley © 2004. For further information see www.dkimages.com
Dorling Kindersley Ltd., 80 Strand, London WC2R ORL

Contents

Introduction	4
A Look Beneath the Surface	9
Riding the Rock Cycle	15
Finding Facts From Fossils	20
Dating Planet Earth	24
The Earth's Story	32
A Continuing Quest	37
Glossary	38
Index	40

Introduction

Humans have asked questions about the land around them for thousands of years. What is the Earth made of? What makes the ground quake and volcanoes erupt? How can there be seashells on mountain peaks? Over the years we have made many discoveries about our planet by studying rocks.

There are many reasons to find out about the Earth. Humans have long used rocks and minerals – from the simplest stone tools to metals used to build intricate machinery – to make life easier. By learning about the processes that shape our planet, scientists can try to prevent the destruction caused by earthquakes and volcanoes.

Humans are curious, too. As we study the evidence of past events in rocks – the rock record – we discover clues about the Earth's history. We can begin to understand how our planet and the life it supports have changed over time.

early stone axe with a flint head

The Paria Wilderness Area in Arizona, United States, is made up of sedimentary rock that has been laid down over millions of years.

Sedimentary rock is deposited in layers.

Spinning Tales

For thousands of years, people all over the world told stories to explain what they could not understand. When the ancient Greeks dug up fossils of animals that no longer existed, they must have wondered where such strange creatures came from.

One such fossil is of *Deinotherium giganteum*, an animal related to the elephant. The skull, found on the Greek island of Crete, has a large opening in the centre. This might have inspired tales of the one-eyed giant, Cyclops.

It was not until the sixteenth century that people began to use science to try to answer their questions. The scientific method of questioning, observing and experimenting has provided insights into the history of our planet.

The fictional Greek character, Odysseus, is fighting a Cyclops.

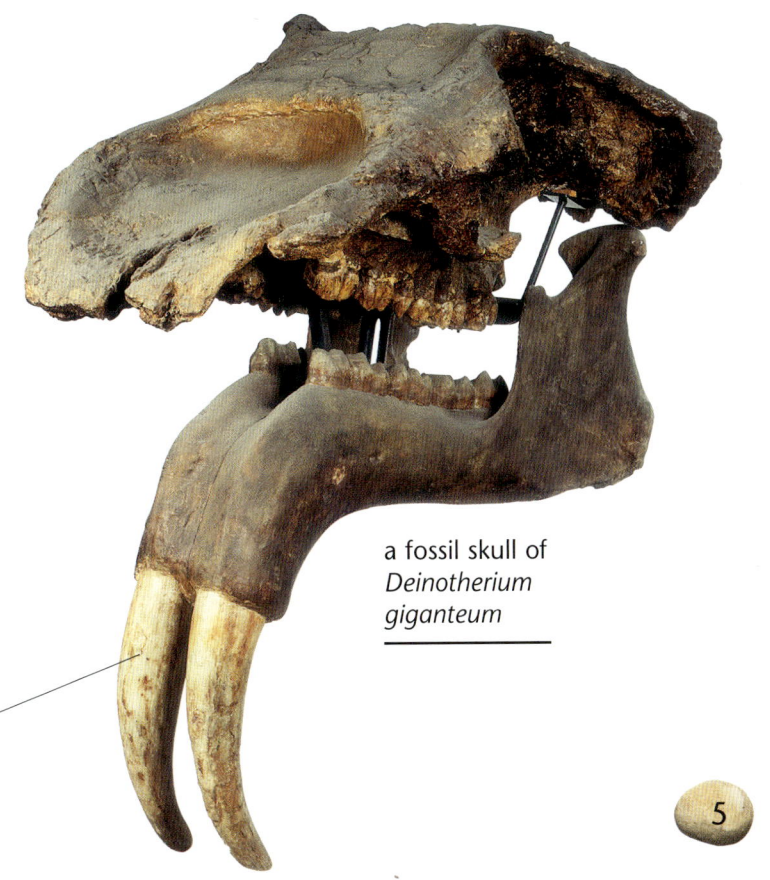

a fossil skull of *Deinotherium giganteum*

long tusks

What Is Geology?

Geology is the science that seeks to understand our planet through its rocks. Geologists study all parts of the Earth, from the top of mountains to the bottom of the ocean floor.

The Earth is always changing. Some changes, such as a powerful earthquake, can be felt. Other changes can only be detected by scientific instruments. Some changes are quick, such as the hot fury of a volcanic eruption. Others, such as the slow growth of a mountain range, take millions of years.

Trans Hex diamond mine in South Africa contains a reddish soil that is full of diamonds.

Geologists study mounds called stromatolites on the seabed. They are formed by algae and some are as old as 3.5 billion years.

Many Types of Geology

Geology is divided into many areas. Petrologists study rocks – what they are made of and where they came from. Seismologists study earthquakes. They look for clues to what goes on below the surface before earthquakes happen. They also measure an earthquake's power and intensity.

Volcanologists want to know what volcanoes can reveal about how the Earth was formed and how it changes today. Historical geologists study how the Earth has changed since it formed more than 4.6 billion years ago. Palaeontologists focus on the history of life on Earth. They use clues found in rocks to learn about animals that lived long ago.

Volcanologists take samples of molten lava from volcanoes to learn what happens deep inside Earth.

This fossil is an example of the remains of a creature that once lived in the sea.

Tools of the Trade

For years, geologists used microscopes and chemicals as well as picks, mallets, hammers and other tools to study rocks. Nowadays they use computers and tools that measure the motion of atoms to record and process data that humans could not observe otherwise.

Using these modern tools and scientific techniques, geologists continue to uncover the rich history of our ever-changing planet.

Geologists use trowels and brushes to clear soil away from rocks. They sieve the soil for small particles of fossils and rock.

High-Tech Tools

Technology has given scientists new ways to examine rock samples and geological processes.

Seismographs measure shock waves in the Earth. Then they plot the shock waves on a graph.

Acceleration mass spectrometers measure how quickly certain particles in rocks decay. They are useful for measuring the age of rocks.

Electron microscopes use electrons instead of light to "illuminate" an object for closer study. Because electron waves are smaller than light waves, they can provide finer detail than a microscope.

a seismograph

A Look Beneath the Surface

Geologists can take samples from only a short distance beneath the Earth's surface. Geologists use their knowledge about what happens in the top layer, the **crust**, to think about what happens deeper down.

At the centre of our planet is a hot, dense **inner core** of iron. It reaches temperatures between 3,000 degrees and 5,000 degrees Celsius. A liquid **outer core** surrounds this mainly iron centre.

The layer above the outer core is called the **mantle**. The mantle forms almost 80 per cent of the total volume of the Earth. Though the mantle is mostly solid, the top is partly molten and composed of superheated liquid rock called magma. Above the mantle, the crust ranges in depth from 4 to 60 kilometres.

The layers beneath the surface of Earth.

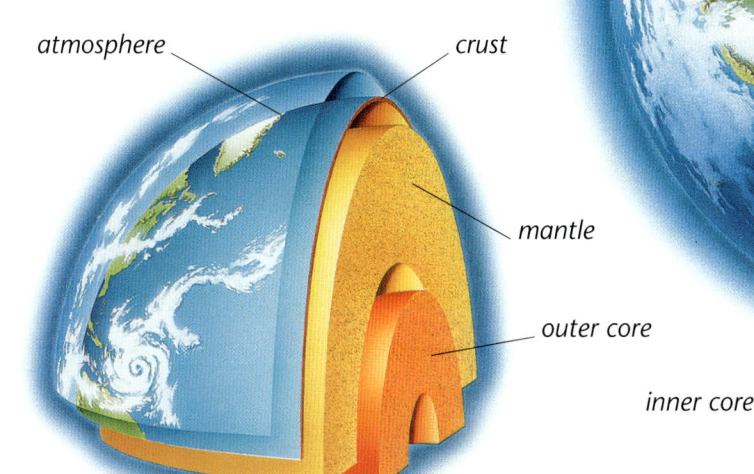

atmosphere
crust
mantle
outer core
inner core

The Lithosphere and Tectonic Plates

Both the **crust** and the rocky outer part of the **mantle** can move around on the Earth's surface. These layers of crust and outer mantle, are called the **lithosphere**. The lithosphere covers the entire Earth, though it is broken up into large sheets of thick rock called **tectonic plates**. The layer underneath the lithosphere is called the **asthenosphere**. This is made up of partly liquid rock which allows the tectonic plates to move. There are two types of tectonic plates: continental and oceanic. The continents of the Earth are deeply embedded into continental plates. Oceanic plates lie beneath the seafloor.

Geologists have mapped out the plates that make up the lithosphere.

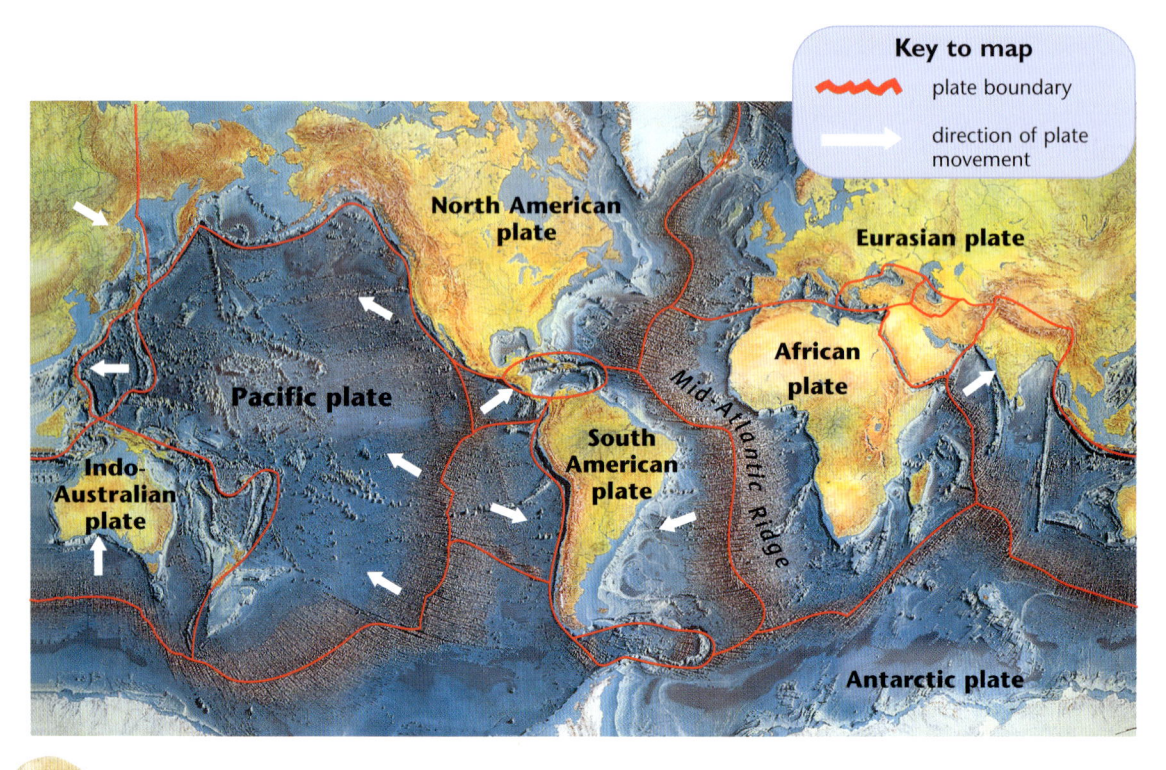

Key to map
- plate boundary
- direction of plate movement

North American plate
Eurasian plate
Pacific plate
African plate
Mid-Atlantic Ridge
Indo-Australian plate
South American plate
Antarctic plate

Seven large plates and many smaller ones float on the molten rock of the mantle. The hot, thick liquid slowly churns, so the plates are in constant motion. This movement of tectonic plates is one of the forces that has shaped our Earth.

Continental Drift

Early in the twentieth century, Alfred Wegener, a German meteorologist, developed the theory of continental drift. This theory says that continents change position on the Earth's surface as the plates on which they rest move.

According to this theory, more than 200 million years ago all the continents on our planet may have been part of one huge landmass, called Pangaea (pan-JEE-uh).

Over time, the movement of the tectonic plates gradually pulled this supercontinent apart. Pangaea split into smaller pieces. The pieces drifted apart and formed our modern continents.

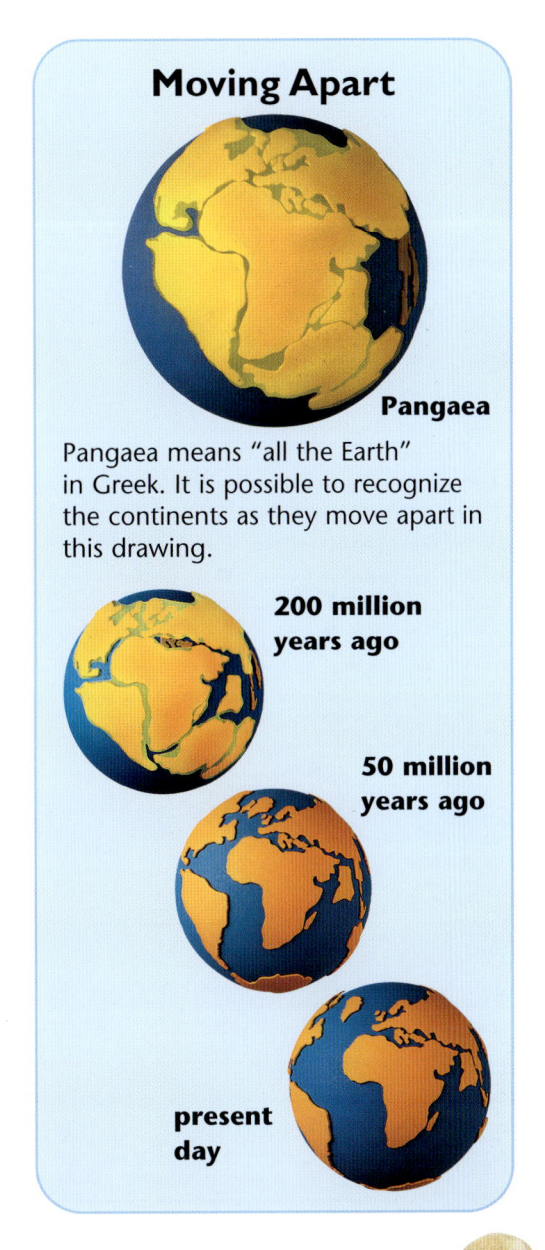

Moving Apart

Pangaea

Pangaea means "all the Earth" in Greek. It is possible to recognize the continents as they move apart in this drawing.

200 million years ago

50 million years ago

present day

The Shaking Earth

Tectonic plates slide against each other, push against each other or pull away from each other. These movements crack and fold the Earth's crust near the edge of the plates. A break in the crust along which plates move is called a fault. Earthquakes occur along faults.

As plates slide, tremendous forces builds up as they push past each other, until rock along the fault slips. This sends out vibrations called seismic waves. The seismic waves signal that an earthquake has occurred. Many quakes are so slight that people do not notice them. However, **seismographs** can measure these plate movements.

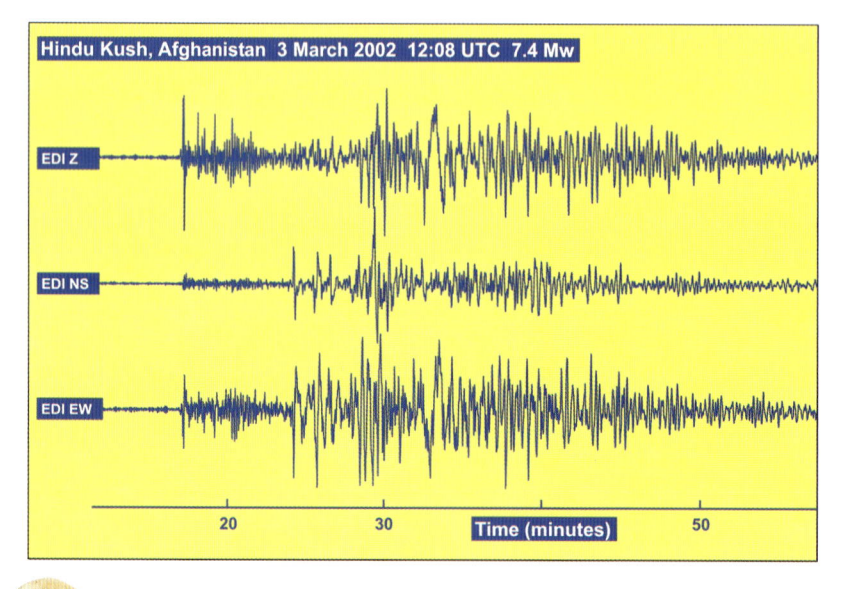

The San Andreas fault line in California, United States, has been created by the Pacific Ocean plate grinding past the North American plate.

Earthquakes are measured according to the Richter scale.

The movement of tectonic plates is also responsible for the formation of mountains. Mountains can form in several different ways.

Volcanic Mountains

Volcanic mountains form mainly at the edges of tectonic plates. They can also form over hot spots caused by plumes of magma (molten rock) deep within the **mantle**. The volcanoes of the Hawaiian Islands were formed when a plate passed over such a hot spot. The magma made its way towards the surface of the Earth's **crust** and formed the volcanoes. It forced its way up through solid rock and poured out through an opening called a vent.

Magma erupting from Earth creates volcanic mountains.

Some Common Volcano Types

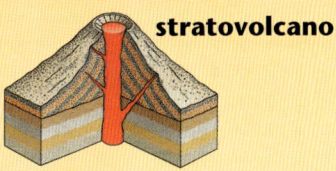

stratovolcano

Stratovolcanoes, or composite volcanoes, are often cone-shaped. They are formed by repeated explosive eruptions of magma.

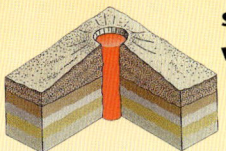

shield volcano

Shield volcanoes are so-called because they are thought to look like a broad, sloped warrior's shield. They are formed when lava flows for kilometres without cooling.

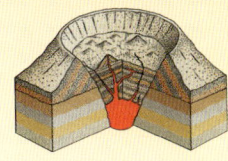

caldera volcano

Caldera volcanoes have a large, round, sunken area at the top. They form when magma erupts with enough force to collapse the ground underneath.

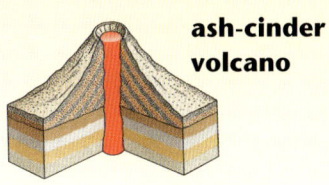

ash-cinder volcano

Cinder cones, also cone-shaped, have very steep sides. They are made from cinders of lava, or magma that has emerged from the volcano, and are often formed in one violent eruption.

Fault-Block Mountains

fault

Fault-block mountains are formed when two **tectonic plates** jostle against each other. Massive blocks of rock called horsts are gradually lifted between faults formed by plate movements. These horsts are called fault-block mountains.

Tectonic plates can rub in three directions: horizontal, vertical and oblique (any sort of diagonal direction). This is why fault-block mountains are different shapes.

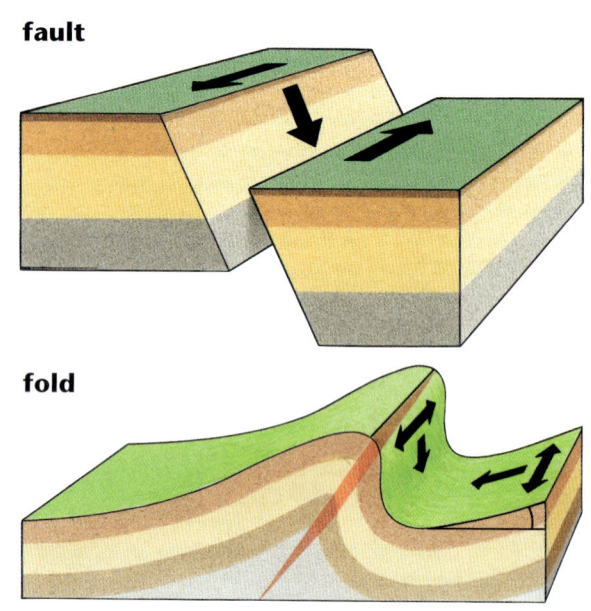

fold

Faults and folds, both created by the movements of tectonic plates, form different types of mountains.

Folded Mountains

Folded mountains form when one plate buckles and folds over another as they push against each other. Folded mountains can be as small as a hill or as large as a huge mountain range. The Himalayas is a folded mountain range that started to form when the continental plates of Asia and India began to collide about 50 million years ago.

The Himalayas range in south Asia was formed when a plate carrying India collided with the Eurasian plate.

Riding the Rock Cycle

Geologists study how rocks form. The **rock cycle** is the term used to describe how old rocks transform into new ones. There are three major categories of rock: **igneous** (IG-nee-uhs) **rock**, **sedimentary rock** and **metamorphic rock**.

Weathering, chemical reactions, pressure and heat are involved in the rock cycle. Weathering grinds rocks into smaller particles that can form new rock. Chemical reactions and pressure can change the minerals in rock. Heat can melt rock and reform it.

The Rock Cycle

Igneous rock is weathered and eroded.

Volcano erupts lava and ash.

Ash and grains of rock form in layers.

igneous rock

Some sedimentary and metamorphic rock wears away to form new layers.

Magma rises and erupts as lava.

Igneous rock forms when erupted lava cools.

sedimentary rock

Igneous rock forms when magma cools under ground.

Rock melts to form magma.

Heat and pressure recrystallize rock into other rock.

metamorphic rock

Rock may melt to make new magma.

igneous rock

The **igneous rocks** pumice and obsidian have the same chemical composition. The differences in their appearance are due to the way they form.

pumice floating on water

obsidian, a natural glass

Igneous Rock

Granite and basalt are examples of igneous rocks. They are formed from magma in the **mantle**. Igneous rocks are the building blocks of the Earth. Magma moves from the upper mantle and lower **crust**, then cools into igneous rock. Geologists classify different types of igneous rocks by their colour and texture, their mineral composition and where they formed.

The Cullin Hills in the Isle of Skye, Scotland, contain different igneous rocks, including gabbro, granite and basalt.

Cooling Off

Magma that reaches the surface of the Earth while it is still liquid cools and solidifies quickly. Igneous rocks that form this way are called extrusive.

When magma begins to cool before it reaches the surface it solidifies slowly. The extra time allows minerals to form into crystals. The longer it takes magma to solidify, the more time there is for crystals to form. These types of igneous rocks are classified as intrusive. Valuable minerals often form in spaces in intrusive igneous rock.

pyrite

gold in quartz

Slow cooling allows the minerals in magma to form crystals.

quartz

amethyst

emerald

Quartz

The quartz crystals in an igneous rock can be small or large, depending on how quickly the rock cooled. Quartz can be any shade between clear and purple. Amethyst is a quartz that is purple. The difference in colour is because of minerals or other impurities in the quartz such as iron oxide.

Sedimentary Rock

Sedimentary rock is formed by layers of different rocks. Wind and rain break down rock into very small pieces. Over time these loose bits of rock gather and settle to form layers of **sediment**.

Over millions of years, layers of sediment are pressed together into rock. Conglomerate looks like a handful of rounded pebbles glued together. It forms on beaches or in rivers. Sandstone is another common sedimentary rock. It forms from small particles of sand. Shale and mudstone are made from tiny grains of silt or clay.

Some sedimentary rocks can form from chemicals dissolved in rainwater. Rock salt and gypsum are examples. Other sedimentary rocks, such as most limestone, are made mainly from the remains of living things.

limestone

Sedimentary rocks may not look alike, but they are created by the same process.

conglomerate

red sandstone

The Grand Canyon in Arizona, United States, is an example of how weathering has shaped rocks.

breccia violetto

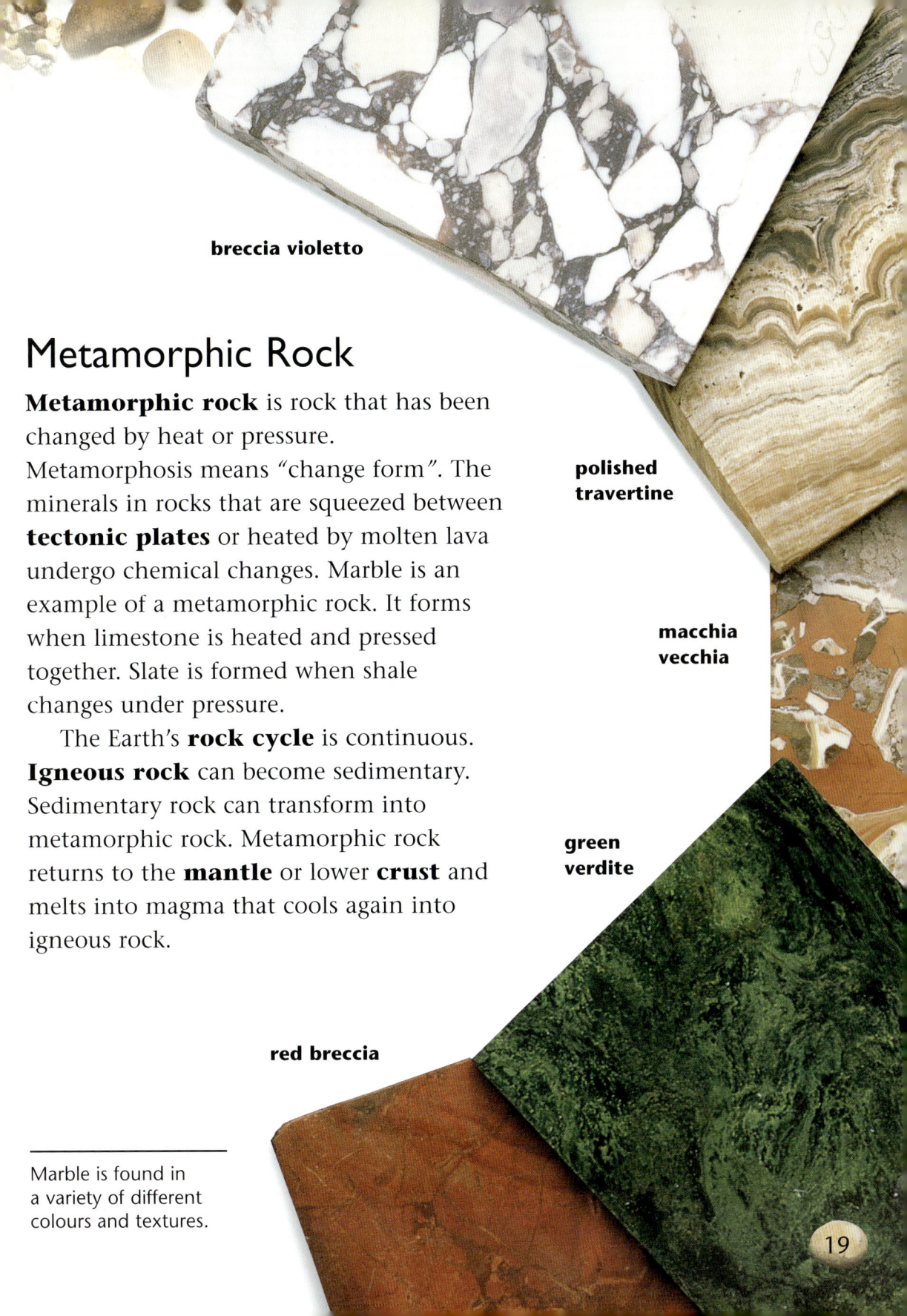

Metamorphic Rock

Metamorphic rock is rock that has been changed by heat or pressure. Metamorphosis means "change form". The minerals in rocks that are squeezed between **tectonic plates** or heated by molten lava undergo chemical changes. Marble is an example of a metamorphic rock. It forms when limestone is heated and pressed together. Slate is formed when shale changes under pressure.

The Earth's **rock cycle** is continuous. **Igneous rock** can become sedimentary. Sedimentary rock can transform into metamorphic rock. Metamorphic rock returns to the **mantle** or lower **crust** and melts into magma that cools again into igneous rock.

polished travertine

macchia vecchia

green verdite

red breccia

Marble is found in a variety of different colours and textures.

Finding Facts From Fossils

Fossils are the remains or other evidence (such as footprints or teeth marks) of plants or animals preserved in rock. Dead plants and animals fell to the bottom of the marshes, lakes and the sea. If they were covered by **sediment** they did not rot away but formed fossils.

This trilobite cast shows how fossilization preserves the details of creatures long dead.

This glossopteris fossil is an ancient fern leaf. Many of these fossils are found across the southern hemisphere in what was the supercontinent of Gondwanaland.

Trace Fossils

Many plants and animals are fossilized as trace fossils. Trace fossils include moulds and casts. A mould forms when the shape of an animal or plant is left in soft sediment that hardens into rock, while a cast forms when a mould fills up with sediment and hardens. These can give us a detailed record of many kinds of organisms.

These are moulds of footprints from two early humans made 3.6 million years ago in volcanic ash in Tanzania.

Permineralization

Harder materials can fossilize in a different way. Materials such as wood, bone and shell contain tiny holes. Minerals from water slowly fill the holes and crystals begin to form inside. The original material keeps its shape. This process is called permineralization.

Sometimes the minerals replace most or all of the original material. This process is called **petrifaction**, which means "change to stone". A piece of petrified wood feels as heavy as a rock, but still looks like wood.

Between 135 and 200 million years ago, this coral lived in a warm, shallow reef. Coral, like wood and bone, is frequently found permineralized.

The Petrified Forest National Park, Arizona, United States, contains the fossilized remains of 225-million-year-old trees.

21

The Tiniest Fossils

Microfossils, less than 1 milllimetre across, may be too small to see without a microscope. They are often found in rocks brought up from the depths of the Earth by drilling.

Micro-organisms, such as bacteria, are the oldest forms of life to leave a fossil record. Spores and pollen from the earliest plant life have been preserved as microfossils, although the plants they came from may not have fossilized. Scanning under an electron microscope can reveal the tiniest details of microfossils and can give important information about what types of early life existed on Earth and how they evolved.

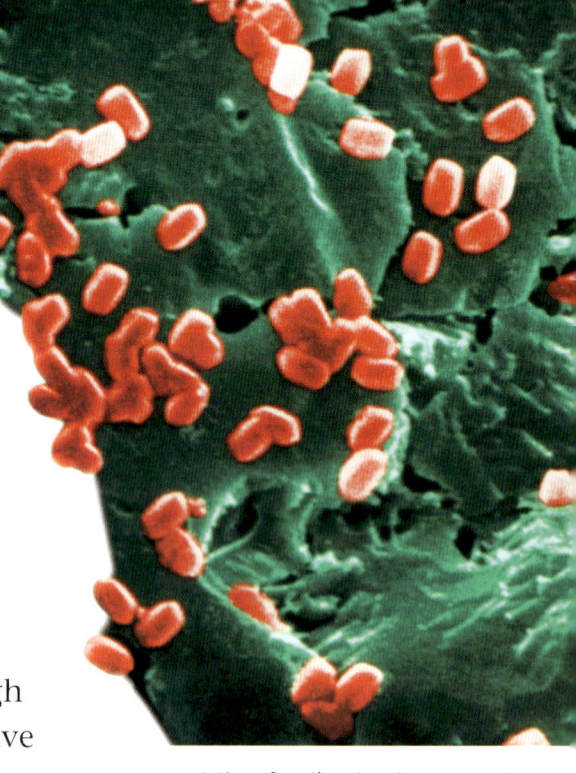

Microfossils give important information about early life on our planet.

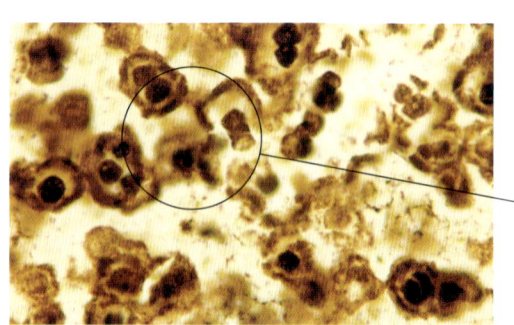

These 2-billion-year-old microfossils, found in Ontario, Canada, are the earliest evidence of life found so far.

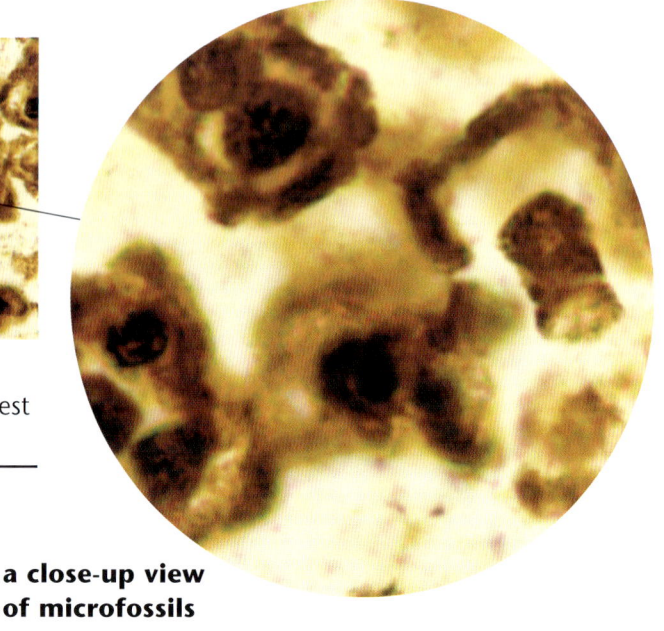

a close-up view of microfossils

Trapped in the resin of a prehistoric plant that hardened into amber, this spider still looks ready to take its next step after waiting millions of years.

Fixed in Time

Amber is fossilized plant sap or resin. Tiny prehistoric creatures are sometimes preserved in amber. These creatures were trapped on the sticky surface of an ancient plant or tree, and then they were covered with even more resin. The resin hardened into amber, preserving the finest details of the trapped creatures.

Plants are preserved as fossils when leaves and stems are quickly buried and flattened. As **sediment** layers form above the trapped plant, the pressure builds. The leaves and stem are squeezed into a thin carbon film, making a "fossil photograph" of a plant.

This ancient maple seed has been perfectly preserved as a fossil.

Coal is a very common form of carbonized prehistoric plant life.

Dating Planet Earth

It is possible to discover when life began and how Earth and the life it supports have changed over the years. Events on Earth have left clues. Geologists and palaeontologists (scientists who study fossils) work together to learn as much as they can. As they decipher rock and fossil records, we gain an understanding of how life has developed and changed.

When fossils of extinct sea animals, such as trilobites, are found on mountain peaks, scientists can see how the Earth has changed.

This artist's impression of life on the seabed 530 million years ago is based on information from the Burgess Shale, an important fossil site in the Canadian Rockies.

Relative Dating

In the nineteenth century, William Smith, an English engineer, saw that undisturbed layers of rock, or strata, carry a portrait of the Earth's history.

He realized that when strata are undisturbed, the bottom layer of a rock bed is normally the oldest layer. Each successive layer of rock forms later, on top of the layer beneath. Understanding which layers were laid down when makes it possible to compare the age of fossils found in the rock bed. Any fossil found in a lower layer of rock would be older than fossils found in the upper strata. This form of dating rock layers and the fossils found in them is called **relative dating**.

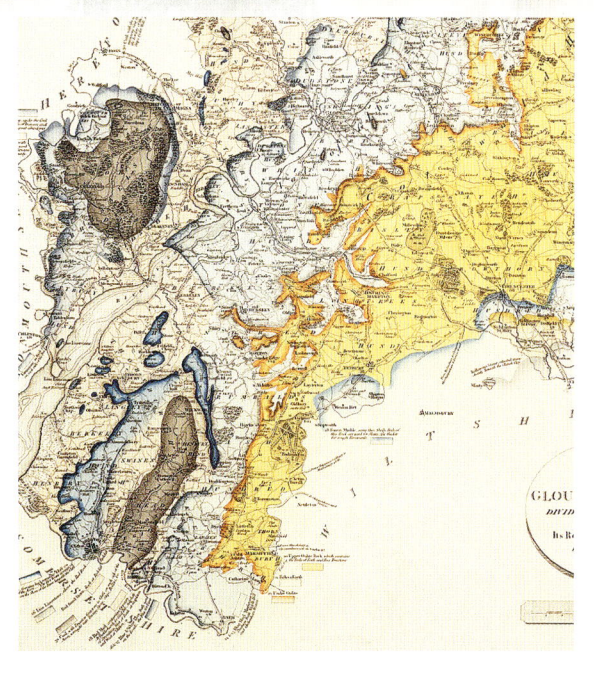

This section of a map of Gloucestershire, drawn by William Smith, indicates the geological ages he discovered.

rocks tilt at different angles

Strata are not always formed in simple, straight layers.

disturbance in the layered sequence of rock

Index Fossils

Relative dating also provides a way to compare information from different locations. Rocks that contain the same species of fossils, even if they are in different types of rocks or far apart in the world, may well have developed during the same time.

Fossils of species found in several layers of rock strata can tell us about broad periods of time. Other fossils, called **index fossils**, give us information about the specific strata in which they are found. These fossils can help us estimate the age of a rock layer or the environment in which it was formed. The presence of an index fossil in different rock strata, for instance, shows they are the same age, even if they are different types of rock.

ediacara

Single-celled blue-green algae are the first organisms known. They developed from about 4,000 million years ago.

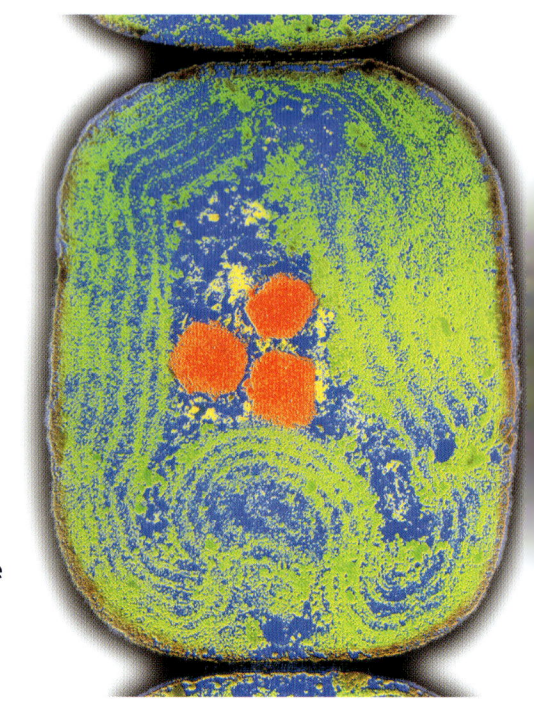

highly magnified image of blue-green algae, still living today

To be useful as an index fossil, a species must have evolved quickly and it must have become extinct in a short period. An index fossil must also come from an easily identified creature or plant whose remains are widely distributed in different locations. Trilobites, shelled animals that once lived in the sea, are useful as index fossils. They are found only in rocks aged between 250 million and 570 million years old.

Fossils provide scientists with a great deal of information. However, they usually cannot tell the exact age of a **sedimentary** layer. To establish an exact age, geologists use nearby **igneous rocks**.

trilobite

Trilobites flourished as swimmers, crawlers and burrowers in shallow seas.

Ammonites were squid-like shellfish that lived 65 million to 250 million years ago.

ammonite

giant cerith

Gastropods, such as snails, first appear in the fossil record about 65 million years ago.

Geological Rock Column

era	million years ago
Cenozoic era	
	65
Mesozoic era	
	250
Palaeozoic era	
	570
Precambrian time	
	4,600

This geological rock column shows the four main eras into which Earth history is divided.

Radiometric Dating

Assigning an age in actual years is called **absolute dating**. This process was not possible until the discovery of radioactivity in the late nineteenth century. Dating objects by their radioactivity is called radiometric dating. This process can date even the oldest rocks on Earth.

Scientists have divided the ages of Earth into four main eras. The earliest is the **Precambrian era**, which started about 4,600 million years ago. Time from about 570 million years ago to the present is divided into three eras. The **Palaeozoic era** lasted from about 570 to 250 million years ago. The **Mesozoic era** lasted from about 250 to 65 million years ago and the **Cenozoic era** started about 65 million years ago and is still continuing.

In radiometric dating, scientists compare different types of radioactive elements in a rock, to establish how old it is. However, it can be complicated and is not always accurate. For example, dating **sedimentary rocks** that are made up of weathered **igneous rocks** would tell when the original igneous rocks were formed. It wouldn't tell us when the sedimentary rock was laid down.

Another form of radiometric dating called radiocarbon dating is used to date the remains of animals, plants and humans that lived in the last 70,000 years.

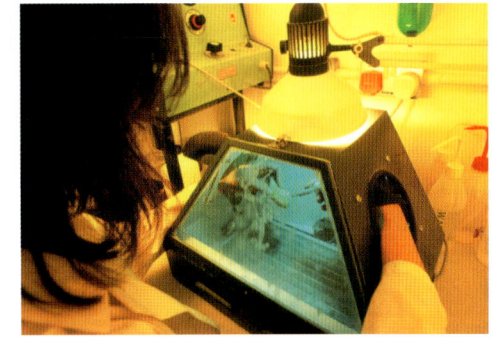

Samples need to be carefully cleaned in a laboratory before they can be radiocarbon dated.

Radiocarbon dating determined that a volcano erupted 6,640 years ago to create Crater Lake in Oregon, USA.

Using Absolute and Relative Dating

A set of rock layers containing a unique group of fossils is called a zone. When geologists study the fossil record in a particular zone, they can determine which creatures lived and died during a certain period. By using radiometric dating on **igneous rocks** in the same zone, geologists can determine the absolute age of the surrounding rocks. Using **absolute** and **relative dating** in fossil zones around the world has helped geologists construct a more accurate picture of the Earth's history.

Igneous and **sedimentary rocks** in the same strata can be used to date **index fossils**.

Scientists use a mass spectrometer to determine the age of a sample through radiocarbon dating.

Other Dating Methods

New techniques are being developed to gather geological information. Using different methods can confirm dates and help scientists obtain a clear picture of how the Earth and life on it has changed. The layers of silt, sand and clay deposited by glaciers are examined to determine the composition of rocks and the climate of an area over time. Tree rings and fossilized pollen are also studied to date fossil zones more accurately.

Geologists continue to seek new methods to classify and date the huge numbers of fossils. From them, we are getting a picture of the Earth's history, backed by solid scientific evidence found in the rock records.

This fossilized conifer grain, called *Corollina,* has been magnified 1,600 times using a scanning electron microscope.

Scientists bore through the ice to take deep cylindrical cores. They study the cores under powerful microscopes.

Earth's Story

Billions of years ago, as the newly formed Earth cooled into a ball of rock and metal, huge volcanic eruptions spewed ash and gases into the air. Clouds formed from the floating ash, shading the Earth from the direct heat of the Sun.

Changes took place as the planet cooled. Oceans formed and an atmosphere grew. The young Earth was a world of violent lightning storms and volcanic eruptions. It was a vastly different place from the home we know. All of these physical and chemical forces combined and reacted over many millions of years.

Small mammals appeared.

Dinosaurs became extinct.

Global mountain building occurred.

Soft-bodied animals appeared (eg worms and jellyfish).

Trilobites appeared.

PRECAMBRIAN

PALAEOZOIC ERA

Organisms appeared (eg blue-green algae).

Earth formed.

Coral reefs appeared.

Marine plants flourished.

Land plants appeared.

Vertebrates appeared.

More complex types of algae appeared.

Geological time

This geological time scale shows the ages of Earth and when different life-forms appeared.

Flowering plants appeared.

Birds appeared.

Dinosaurs flourished.

Marine reptiles appeared.

MESOZOIC ERA

Oil and gas deposits formed.

Himalayas began to form.

Early deserts occurred.

Amphibians appeared.

Large mammals appeared.

PALAEOZOIC

Conifers appeared.

CENOZOIC ERA

Humans appeared.

The Earliest Time

The history of the Earth shown on page 28 is broken into different eras based on the types of life that existed in them. The **Precambrian era** is the earliest era, and its life is the least well known because few fossils exist. During this time, life-forms evolved, or changed over time, from organisms with a single cell to more complex, multi-celled plants and animals. Such soft organisms left few clues behind to tell their story, although some fossils were formed.

Life Blooms: The Palaeozoic Era

The **Palaeozoic era** began 570 million years ago and ended about 250 million years ago. During the Palaeozoic era, life evolved from more primitive organisms into animals, such as trilobites, sharks and cockroaches. This development happened slowly, in stages.

Fossil records show that vast seas covered much of the ancient Earth at times. Plant life evolved first in the oceans, along with many animal species. The seas receded and rose, again and again. Plants began to grow on the Earth's surface. These plants eventually evolved into huge forests. When the Earth had an atmosphere that could support animal life, the first amphibians left the water to live on land, at least some of the time.

Fish with jaws first developed in the Palaeozoic era.

These giant tree ferns in New Zealand's Otari reserve are very similar to the landscape in the Palaeozoic era.

The Age of Dinosaurs: The Mesozoic Era

The **Mesozoic era** started about 250 million years ago and ended about 65 million years ago. This is the period when dinosaurs evolved, ruling the planet for more than 150 million years. The first birds took flight during this era, and the earliest mammals also evolved. These early mammals were small, and had little chance of competing with dinosaurs. However, at the end of the Mesozoic era, dinosaurs vanished and mammals thrived.

It's possible that a meteor strike caused the disappearance of the dinosaurs. Dust from the impact might have dimmed the sunlight, changing the climate of the Earth and killing the plants that dinosaurs ate. Rock records support this theory. A thin layer of clay has been found in rocks formed at the end of the Mesozoic era. This clay is rich in an element that is not usually found on the Earth's surface, but is plentiful in meteorites. The clay layers might have formed after an enormous meteorite slammed into the Earth.

allosaurus skull

Fossilized skeletal remains, such as this skull, give geologists the information they need to reconstruct how dinosaurs probably looked.

reconstruction of an allosaurus

Glaciers and Mammals: The Cenozoic Era

The **Cenozoic era** is the time of mammals: animals that have hair, feed their young with milk and are warm-blooded. Mammals have large brains compared to other animals of the same size. The fossil record in this era shows the development of familiar mammals and the rise of *Homo sapiens*, or humans.

Glaciers – thick sheets of ice – spread over the Earth during part of the Cenozoic era. The glaciers advanced and retreated many times. As glaciers bridged the continents and sea levels changed, humans migrated across the Earth. By testing bones and belongings, the timing of these migrations, and of the activity of the glaciers, can be discovered.

As glaciers covered Earth, animals were occasionally trapped in swampy areas and frozen. Ice preserved this mammoth for at least 12,000 years.

The giant Moai statues on Easter Island in the Pacific Ocean were carved out of volcanic rock by people 1,200 years ago.

A Continuing Quest

Although geologists and other scientists who study the Earth have answered many questions about our planet, there are many more questions to answer. Scientists continue to work together to understand the processes that shape our planet. Whether it's a volcano blowing its top, a sandstorm weathering rock, an earthquake shaking a city or just a simple stream smoothing its bed, you can see the processes that have shaped the Earth for billions of years.

Geologists are constantly studying movements within the Earth to anticipate and prepare for natural disasters, such as earthquakes.

Are You Interested in Geology?

Amateur geologists and palaeontologists have made many important finds. The best way to get started with rock and fossil hunting is to contact collectors who are familiar with an area. They will be able to suggest tools and recommend sites where the best specimens might be found.

Safety equipment is important. Sturdy shoes, a hard hat, goggles and gloves will provide protection. Carry a first-aid kit, maps and a compass, and always go with an adult who knows the area. Be sure to take a camera to record discoveries made while you study our fascinating planet.

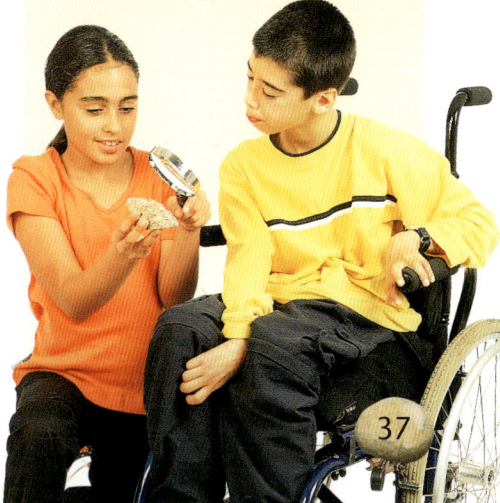

Glossary

absolute dating — the assignment of a specific age to a rock, fossil or other object

asthenosphere — a partly molten layer near the edge of the Earth's mantle, below the lithosphere

Cenozoic era — the most recent of the four major classifications of geologic time, including the present, when mammals evolved into a rich variety of species

crust — the thin outer layer of the Earth's surface

fault-block mountains — mountains created by movements along faults

folded mountains — mountains of varying sizes created by one tectonic plate buckling under another

igneous rock — rock formed from cooled magma

index fossils — fossils from a species known to have existed during a particular span of geologic time

inner core — the dense, mainly iron, centre of the Earth

lithosphere — the outer layer of the Earth, made up of the crust and the outer part of the mantle

mantle — the semi-solid rock layer between the Earth's outer core and its crust, comprising almost 80 per cent of the total volume of the planet

Mesozoic era — the third oldest of the four major classifications of geologic time, when dinosaurs dominated Earth

metamorphic rock — rock that is formed from other rock by heat, pressure or other chemical changes

outer core — a liquid layer made up mostly of molten iron surrounding the Earth's inner core

Palaeozoic era	the second oldest of the four major divisions of geologic time, a time of expansion and evolution of many life-forms
petrifaction	process by which minerals replace organic material, and the material hardens into rock
Precambrian era	the oldest of the four major classifications of geologic time, when the planet formed and simple life-forms came into existence
relative dating	the assignment of an age to a rock or fossil in comparison to other rocks or fossils
rock cycle	the continuous transformation of old rocks into new ones by heat, pressure, weathering and chemical reactions
sedimentary rock	rock that forms as sediment is compressed
sediments	particles of rock deposited by wind, water or glaciers
seismographs	machines used to measure the location and intensity of earthquakes
tectonic plates	large sections of the Earth's lithosphere that move

Index

absolute dating 28, 30
amber 23
carbonization 23
cast (fossil) 20
Cenozoic era 28, 33, 36
continental drift 11
crust 9, 10, 13, 16, 19
crystals 17
dinosaurs 33, 35
earthquake 4, 6, 7, 12, 37
fault 12, 14
fault-block mountains 14
folded mountains 14
fossils 5, 7, 20–23, 24, 25, 26, 27, 30, 31, 33, 34, 35, 36, 37
fossil zones 30, 31
geological time scale 32–33
glaciers 31, 36
horst 14
igneous rock 15, 16–17, 19, 27, 29, 30
index fossils 26–27, 30
inner core 9
lava 13, 15, 19
magma 9, 13, 15, 16, 17, 19
mantle 9, 10, 11, 13, 16, 19
Mesozoic era 28, 33, 35
metamorphic rock 15, 19
microfossils 22

minerals 4, 17, 19, 21
mould (fossil) 20
mountain building 13–14
outer core 9
Paleozoic era 28, 32–33, 34
Pangaea 11
permineralization 21
petrifaction 21
plate tectonics 10–14
Precambrian era 28, 32–33
quartz 17
radiocarbon dating 29, 30
radiometric dating 28–29, 30
relative dating 25, 26, 30
Richter scale 12
rock cycle 15
sediment 18, 20, 23
sedimentary rock 4, 15, 18, 19, 27, 29, 30
seismograph 8, 12
Smith, William 25
strata 25–26
tectonic plates 10–14, 19
volcanic mountains 13
volcanoes 4, 7, 13, 29, 32, 37
Wegener, Alfred 11